The Day the River Caught Fire

How the Cuyahoga River Exploded and Ignited the Earth Day Movement

By BARRY WITTENSTEIN

Illustrated by JESSIE HARTLAND

A PAULA WISEMAN BOOK
SIMON & SCHUSTER BOOKS FOR YOUNG READERS
New York London Toronto Sydney New Delhi

SIMON & SCHUSTER BOOKS FOR YOUNG READERS

An imprint of Simon & Schuster Children's Publishing Division

1230 Avenue of the Americas, New York, New York 10020

Text © 2023 by Barry Wittenstein

Illustration © 2023 by Jessie Hartland

Book design by Alicia Mikles © 2023 by Simon & Schuster, Inc.

The photo of the Cuyahoga River in the backmatter used with permission of Bettman/Getty Images.

SIMON & SCHUSTER BOOKS FOR YOUNG READERS and related marks are trademarks of Simon & Schuster, Inc.

For information about special discounts for bulk purchases, please contact Simon & Schuster Special Sales at 1-866-506-1949 or business@simonandschuster.com.

The Simon & Schuster Speakers Bureau can bring authors to your live event. For more information or to book an event,

contact the Simon & Schuster Speakers Bureau at 1-866-248-3049 or visit our website at www.simonspeakers.com.

The text for this book was set in Walbaum.

The illustrations for this book were rendered in gouache.

Manufactured in China

1122 SCP

First Edition

2 4 6 8 10 9 7 5 3 1

Library of Congress Cataloging-in-Publication Data

Names: Wittenstein, Barry, author. | Hartland, Jessie, illustrator.

Title: The day the river caught fire : how the Cuyahoga River exploded and ignited the Earth Day movement / Barry Wittenstein ; illustrated by Jessie Hartland.

Description: First edition. | New York, New York : Simon & Schuster Books for Young Readers, an imprint of Simon & Schuster Children's Publishing Division, [2022]

"A Paula Wiseman book"—t.p. | Includes bibliographical references. | Audience: Ages 4-8 | Audience: Grades 2-3

Summary: "The true story of how a 1969 fire in one of the most polluted rivers in America helped foster awareness of water pollution and how the river's fate contributed to the environmental movement"

—Provided by publisher.

Identifiers: LCCN 2022007383 (print) | LCCN 2022007384 (ebook) | ISBN 9781534480834 (hardcover) | ISBN 9781534480841 (ebook)

Subjects: LCSH: Oil pollution of rivers, harbors, etc.—Ohio—Cuyahoga River—Juvenile literature. | Environmentalism—United States—Juvenile literature. | Earth day—Juvenile literature.

Classification: LCC TD225.C95 W58 2022 (print) | LCC TD225.C95 (ebook)

DDC 363.7009771/31—dc23/eng/20220808 LC record available at https://lccn.loc.gov/2022007383 LC ebook record available at https://lccn.loc.gov/2022007384

Dedicated to Cyrus Pierce Falk and the millions of children around the world.
Your generation will soon be the caretakers of Mother Earth. Protect her well.

With special thanks to Elizabeth Sams, Susanne Wolff, and Richard Bush.

—B. W.

This one is for my best high school pal, now a professor of environmental science, Dr. Sharon Moran, PhD.

—J. H.

On a sticky and sunny Sunday in the summer of 1969, the Cuyahoga River in Cleveland did something rivers should never do.

It began when sparks from a passing railcar jumped into the water. Normally, sparks like that quickly fizzle out.

But the Cuyahoga was not a normal river with normal water. That's because a thick, gooey layer of sludge, oil, and sewage floated on top.

Instead of fizzing out when the sparks met the oily concoction . . .

KABOOM!

Flames shot high into the sky.

Fire engines and a fire boat arrived and
extinguished the flames within minutes.

Then they returned to their firehouses, and That. Was. That. HO-HUM.

No one was surprised, surprisingly. It's burned before, people said. It'll burn again.

Which was true. Since 1886, it happened thirteen times. In 1912, five people lost their lives. And the 1952 fire caused over a million dollars in damage.

It wasn't always like this.

The Cuyahoga once was beautiful.

The river begins in the north, snakes its way south to Akron, and then wiggles up to Cleveland and Lake Erie.

Over the years along the Cuyahoga's path, Indigenous groups such as the Ottawa tribe, Ojibwa tribe, and Ohio Seneca people went canoeing, swimming, and fishing—and ate what they caught! That's how clean the water was.

Then came the Industrial Revolution.

Factories, steel mills, and slaughterhouses began popping up all along the rivers of cities. The population of the country was growing and moving west. A lot more of everything—from steel for automobiles and skyscrapers to gasoline, food, and clothing—was needed, and fast!

Factories released their waste into the nearby waterways, not caring about the environment or what their slop, slush, gunk, and rubbish did to it.

That's how the Cuyahoga became a toxic soup of wood, metal, chemicals, oil, and even animal body parts.

Soon, the river started to stink, stank, stunk. The fish and plant life died. Scientists declared the river D. E. A. D.

The mighty Cuyahoga didn't flow. It gulped, gurgled, and ooooooooozed.

Workers in the nearby factories were warned: *If you fall in, go straight to the hospital.*
Better to be safe than sorry.

For a long time, nobody cared.
HO-HUM.
It is what it is, people said:
disgusting and gross.
HO-HUM.

But in the 1960s, people, especially young people, started to worry. They began to ask questions, like: "Why can't we have progress *and* a clean environment?"

The morning after the 1969 fire, Cleveland's mayor held a news conference on the banks of the Cuyahoga. He declared war.

On pollution.

His name was Carl Stokes. He was one of the first Black mayors of a major American city.

The days of ho-humming were over, he said. Someone needed to take action! Cleveland had suddenly become a symbol of the nation's pollution crisis. Newspapers and magazines told the story of the exploding river.

Comedians joked about it.

Songwriters wrote songs about it.

FROZEN CUSTARD

menu

Burn on, Cuyahoga, burn on

The proud citizens of Cleveland were angry and embarrassed.

But they were not alone. Rivers in many other industrial cities—like Baltimore, Detroit, and Philadelphia—also burst into flames!

Things were KABOOMING out of control!

clean AIR act

clean WATER act

Congress invited experts to come to Washington, DC, to testify. Mayor Stokes was one of them.

Soon, Congress passed important new laws, like the Clean Air and Clean Water acts.

Within a year, on April 22, 1970, the first Earth Day took place.

More than one hundred thousand people flooded Fifth Avenue in New York City. Twenty million across the country. They carried signs, gave speeches, held hands, and sang songs.

It was a protest.
It was a celebration.
It was the beginning of
a movement.

It was as if someone was shouting with a megaphone from high above:

It worked! People finally opened their ears and eyes. They were tired of holding their noses. They learned that caring for the Earth requires constant attention.

Earth Day has taken place every year since 1970, on April 22. In 1990, the entire world got involved, and it now takes place in almost two hundred countries, with a billion people participating.

¡Feliz día de la Tierra!
Hyvää maan päivää
Nuestro Futuro
EARTH day

The 1969 Cuyahoga River fire helped the country understand that this bright blue marble floating through space is our only home.

But here's the good news for the Cuyahoga:

More than forty species of fish have returned to where it flows into Lake Erie.

True, the river might not be as clean as when Indigenous peoples fished
in it and floated down it . . .

but at least it doesn't go . . .

KABOOM!

AUTHOR'S NOTE

If you're reading this, you still have time to save the planet. But time is running short.

The question is, what can you do to help save it?

In 1969, when the Cuyahoga River ignited, many people suddenly woke up to the dangers of water pollution. "Power to the people" was the mantra of the 1960s. An environmental movement had begun.

Scientists predicted worst-case scenarios unless dramatic changes were made to our laws and lifestyles. Their concerns went well beyond one river, one oil spill, or one factory dumping its toxic waste. The problem was humanity's total disregard for its role in the health of the planet. There were too many poisons leaking into the ground and the oceans. This contaminated the fish and made local water supplies undrinkable. Too much carbon dioxide was being released into the air by burning fossil fuels like gasoline and coal. Breathing polluted air was causing cancer rates to rise. Even more dangerously, carbon dioxide was warming the planet by trapping heat in the atmosphere. Ice caps would melt, scientists feared. Ocean levels would rise. Many species could go extinct. Flooding of coastal cities would force migrations of people. But there was time, the experts agreed. All that was needed was desire and acceptance of the crisis. The science was undeniable.

Tragically and, yes, stupidly, not enough people have heeded the warnings since that June day in Cleveland. Corporations and governments resisted. The science is wrong, they said. Nothing to worry about. Live for today, not for the future.

But today is the future. "Climate change" and "global warming" are issues known to every student. Weather events like earthquakes and hurricanes are more powerful than ever. Just as was forecasted in the 1960s, the ice caps are melting at an alarming rate, wildfires are more devastating than ever, and the destruction of coral reefs and the oceans is accelerating. Carbon dioxide levels are the highest they have ever been. Deforestation in the Brazilian Amazon is robbing the earth of a vital resource for cleansing its air.

Humanity is at a point of no return because of man's ignorance and greed. What other species besides human beings destroys its home? This is not science fiction. This is not a movie. This is the world we have created.

The good news, if there is any, is that new technologies are constantly being developed. Solar power and wind power can replace the burning of coal to produce electricity. And there are new ways to remove plastic from the ocean. But will these technologies work as quickly as we need them to work? How effective are they? How much will they cost? The answers are not clear. But this fact is: in every society, change is led by the young.

If the world still exists as you read this, know that there is time to save the planet. So I ask again. Can you invent new solutions? Can you help inform others? Will you tell corporations you won't buy their products if they value profit over the environment? Will you become educated, concerned citizens to better understand the issues facing the survival of humanity? Are you committed to making sure environmental laws are enforced by elected officials?

That is the challenge for your generation. That is *your* challenge.

But hurry, please. Mother Earth is begging to breathe. It's up to you, my young friends.

What will you do?

ENVIRONMENTAL TIME LINE

1962: Rachel Carson, writer, scientist, and ecologist, publishes her book, *Silent Spring*, about the dangers and consequences of pesticides. Many consider this to be the start of the environmental movement.

1963: President Lyndon B. Johnson signs the first Clean Air Act to regulate and enforce air pollution standards.

1969: In Santa Barbara, California, an oil spill spews more than three million gallons of crude oil into the Pacific Ocean. A thirty-five-mile oil slick kills thousands of wildlife, resulting in a public outcry.

1969: The Cuyahoga River catches fire.

1969: Wisconsin native and United States Senator Gaylord Nelson decides to take action to make environmental protection a national issue. Frustrated by the lack of urgency and inspired by the 1960s activism of the anti-Vietnam war protesters, Nelson joins with Denis Hayes, former student body president of Stanford University, to coordinate a series of teach-ins. Hayes is selected as Earth Day's national coordinator.

1969: *Time* magazine publishes an article about the Cuyahoga River fire; the environmental crisis gains national attention.

1970: First Earth Day. An estimated twenty million people in the United States take part, one in every ten people. More than one hundred thousand people walk down New York City's Fifth Avenue.

1970: Cleveland's mayor, Carl Stokes, appears before Congress to advocate for federal aid for pollution cleanup and stricter controls in his and other cities.

1970: Clean Air Act is amended, and then is amended again in 1990.

1970: President Richard M. Nixon creates the U.S. Environmental Protection Agency. The EPA consolidates federal agencies to ensure regulations protecting the environment are followed.

1972: Astronauts on Apollo 17 take the first image of the entire Earth, the beautiful and fragile planet floating in the vastness of space. The photograph is nicknamed the "Blue Marble" and soon becomes a symbol of the environmental movement. It is one of the most viewed images of all time.

1972: The Clean Water Act is passed and then amended in 1977 and 1987, originally known as the Federal Water Pollution Control Act (1948).

1973: Endangered Species Act is passed.

1990: On Earth Day's twentieth anniversary, two hundred million people in 141 countries take part.

2000: 184 countries around the world celebrate Earth Day.

2016: President Obama signs on to the 2015 Paris Agreement, a legally binding environmental pact adopted by nearly two hundred countries to address global warming.

2019: Activist Greta Thunberg leads a youth movement of millions on a global climate strike to protest the use of fossil fuels.

2019: President Donald Trump announces that the United States intends to withdraw from the Paris Climate Accords on November 5, 2020.

2020: 50th Anniversary of Earth Day.

2021: Under President Biden, the United States rejoins the Paris Climate Accords.

2022: Global record for hottest days in history is set.

TO LEARN MORE

VIDEOS
Protecting the Environment
An Inconvenient Truth (2006) trailer at https://youtu.be/Bu6SE5TYrCM

Earth Day
• *American Experience: Earth Days* trailer at https://youtu.be/FwRNj0Op61I
• "Earth Day 1970 - 2020: 50th Anniversary || Time Will Tell" by the American Museum of Natural History at https://www.youtube.com/watch?v=XBrnnByieL4
• "What is Earth Day?" at https://youtu.be/mmRUAXPAMVE

Cuyahoga River Fire
• "Celebrating the Comeback of the Burning River, 1969–2019" at https://youtu.be/18JpT61rX6A
• "Time to Wake Up: 50th Anniversary of the Cuyahoga River Fire with senators Sherrod Brown and Sheldon Whitehouse" at https://www.youtube.com/watch?v=CswhZi7anv4

ORGANIZATIONS
• American Rivers
    A national river conservation organization whose mission is to protect wild rivers, restore damaged rivers, and conserve clean water for people and nature.
    americanrivers.org

• Earth Day
    Founded in 1970 in the United States, Earth Day Network is now an international organization that works to diversify, educate, and activate the environmental movement worldwide.
    earthday.org

• Earth Justice
    A group of lawyers and policy experts that provide free legal expertise to help protect the environment.
    earthjustice.org

• Global Citizen

Global Citizen is an organization of concerned citizens that takes on the issues of water and sanitation, poverty, sustainability, finance, education, and other problems that affect millions throughout the world. globalcitizen.org/en/

• Water.org

A nonprofit cofounded by Matt Damon and Gary White provides access to safe water and sanitation in developing countries. water.org

HOW TO GET INVOLVED
• What You Can Do earthday.org/take-action-now/

FOR FURTHER READING

Ehrlich, Amy, and Wendell Minor. *Rachel: The Story of Rachel Carson*. HMH Books for Young Readers, 2008.

Geisel, Theodore. *The Lorax*. Random House, 1971.

Lindstrom, Carole, and Michaela Goade. *We Are Water Protectors*. Roaring Brook Press, 2020.

Messner, Kate, and Christopher Silas Neal. *Over And Under The Pond*. Chronicle Books, 2017.

Paul, Miranda, and Elizabeth Zunon. *One Plastic Bag: Isatou Ceesay and the Recycling Women of the Gambia*. Millbrook Press, 2015.

Winter, Jeanette. *Our House Is on Fire: Greta Thunberg's Call to Save the Planet*. Beach Lane Books, 2019.

BIBLIOGRAPHY

"America's Sewage System and the Price of Optimism." *Time*, 1 Aug. 1969.

Newman, Randy. "Burn On." *Sail Away*, Reprise Records, 1972, track 8.

"History of the Area National Park Service." Cuyahoga Valley National Park, last modified November 8, 2021, https://www.nps.gov/cuva/learn/kidsyouth/native-americans.htm.

"Oil Slick Fire Damages 2 River Spans." *Cleveland Plain Dealer*, 23 June 1969, p. 11c.

Stradling, David, and Richard Stradling. *Where the River Burned: Carl Stokes and the Struggle to Save Cleveland*. Cornell University Press, 2015.

Wheeling, Kate, and Max Ufberg. "'The Ocean Is Boiling': The Complete Oral History of the 1969 Santa Barbara Oil Spill." https://psmag.com/news/the-ocean-is-boiling-the-complete-oral-history-of-the-1969 -santa-barbara-oil-spill.

The Cuyahoga River on November 03, 1952

The Cuyahoga River feeds into Lake Erie in Northeast Ohio.